HOLIDAY FAVORITES

Solos and Band Arrangements Correlated with Essential Elements® Band Method

Arranged by ROBERT LONGFIELD, JOHNNIE VINSON, MICHAEL SWEENEY and PAUL LAVENDER

Welcome to Essential Elements Holiday Favorites! There are two versions of each selection in this versatile book. The SOLO version appears in the beginning of each student book. The FULL BAND arrangement of each song follows. The ONLINE RECORDINGS or PIANO ACCOMPANIMENT BOOK may be used as an accompaniment for solo performance. Use these recordings when playing solos for friends and family.

To access audio visit:
www.halleonard.com/mylibrary

Enter Code
1050-8395-0316-8879

ISBN 978-1-5400-2800-6

00870018

Visit Hal Leonard Online at
www.halleonard.com

Contact Us:
Hal Leonard
7777 West Bluemound Road
Milwaukee, WI 53213
Email: info@halleonard.com

In Europe contact:
Hal Leonard Europe Limited
42 Wigmore Street
Marylebone, London, W1U 2RN
Email: info@halleonardeurope.com

In Australia contact:
Hal Leonard Australia Pty. Ltd.
4 Lentara Court
Cheltenham, Victoria, 3192 Australia
Email: info@halleonard.com.au

AULD LANG SYNE

TUBA
Solo

Words by ROBERT BURNS
Traditional Scottish Melody
Arranged by MICHAEL SWEENEY

00870018

FELIZ NAVIDAD

TUBA
Solo

Music and Lyrics by
JOSÉ FELICIANO
Arranged by PAUL LAVENDER

00870018

PARADE OF THE WOODEN SOLDIERS

TUBA
Solo

English Lyrics by BALLARD MacDONALD
Music by LEON JESSEL
Arranged by PAUL LAVENDER

00870018

GOOD KING WENCESLAS

TUBA
Solo

Words by JOHN M. NEALE
Music from PIAE CANTIONES
Arranged by ROBERT LONGFIELD

00870018

PAT-A-PAN
(Willie, Take Your Little Drum)

TUBA
Solo

Words and Music by
BERNARD de la MONNOYE
Arranged by ROBERT LONGFIELD

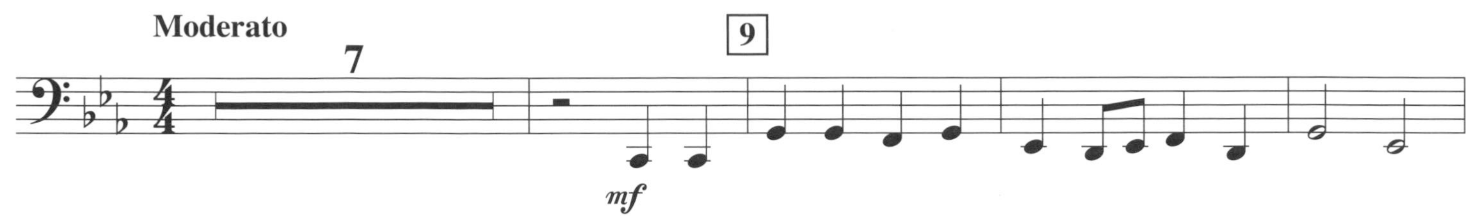

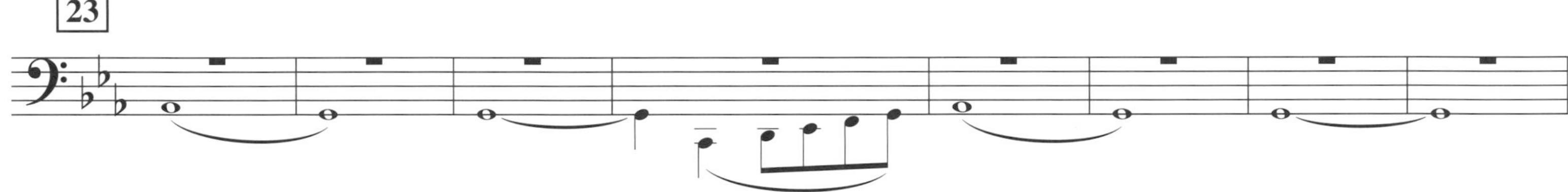

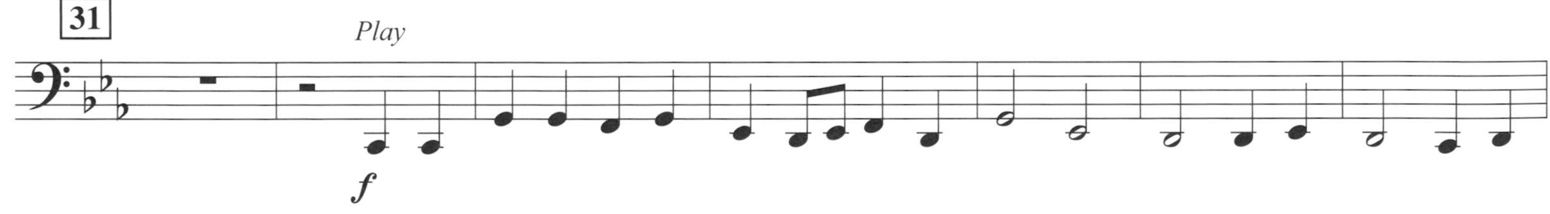

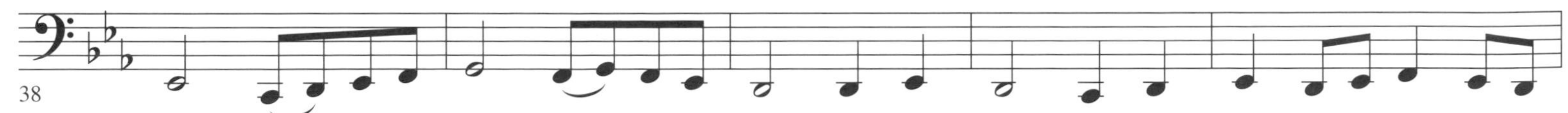

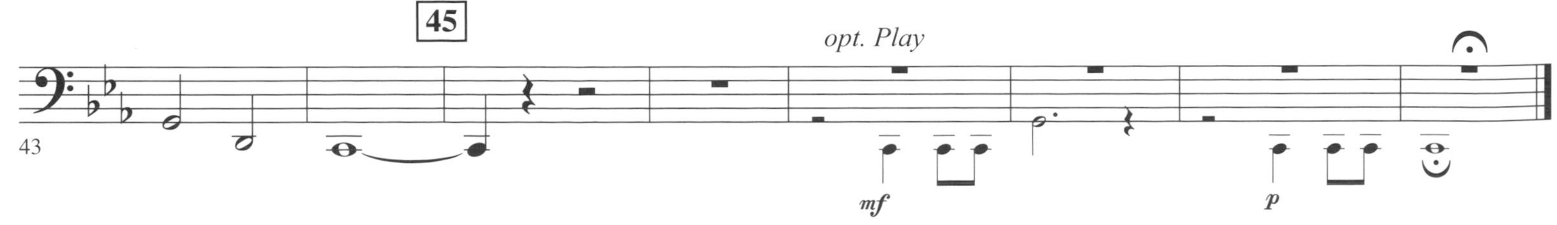

00870018

SILVER BELLS

TUBA
Solo

Words and Music by
JAY LIVINGSTON and RAY EVANS
Arranged by PAUL LAVENDER

00870018

DO YOU HEAR WHAT I HEAR

TUBA
Solo

Words and Music by
NOEL REGNEY and GLORIA SHAYNE
Arranged by MICHAEL SWEENEY

00870018

From THE SOUND OF MUSIC

MY FAVORITE THINGS

TUBA
Solo

Lyrics by OSCAR HAMMERSTEIN II
Music by RICHARD RODGERS
Arranged by ROBERT LONGFIELD

00870018

From the Motion Picture Irving Berlin's HOLIDAY INN

WHITE CHRISTMAS

TUBA
Solo

Words and Music by
IRVING BERLIN
Arranged by JOHNNIE VINSON

00870018

CHRISTMAS TIME IS HERE

TUBA
Solo

Words by LEE MENDELSON
Music by VINCE GUARALDI
Arranged by JOHNNIE VINSON

00870018

From Warner Bros. Pictures' THE POLAR EXPRESS

THE POLAR EXPRESS

TUBA
Solo

Words and Music by
GLEN BALLARD and ALAN SILVESTRI
Arranged by JOHNNIE VINSON

00870018

AULD LANG SYNE

TUBA
Band Arrangement

Words by ROBERT BURNS
Traditional Scottish Melody
Arranged by MICHAEL SWEENEY

12
11
mf

21
16
f
mf

22

29
2
27
f

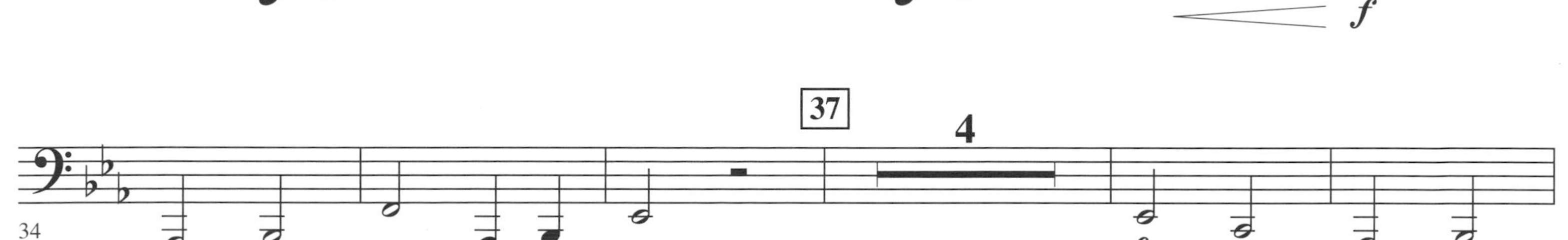

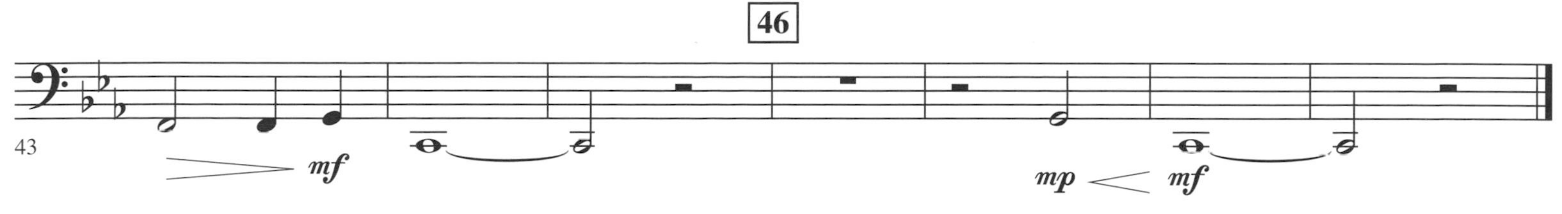

FELIZ NAVIDAD

TUBA
Band Arrangement

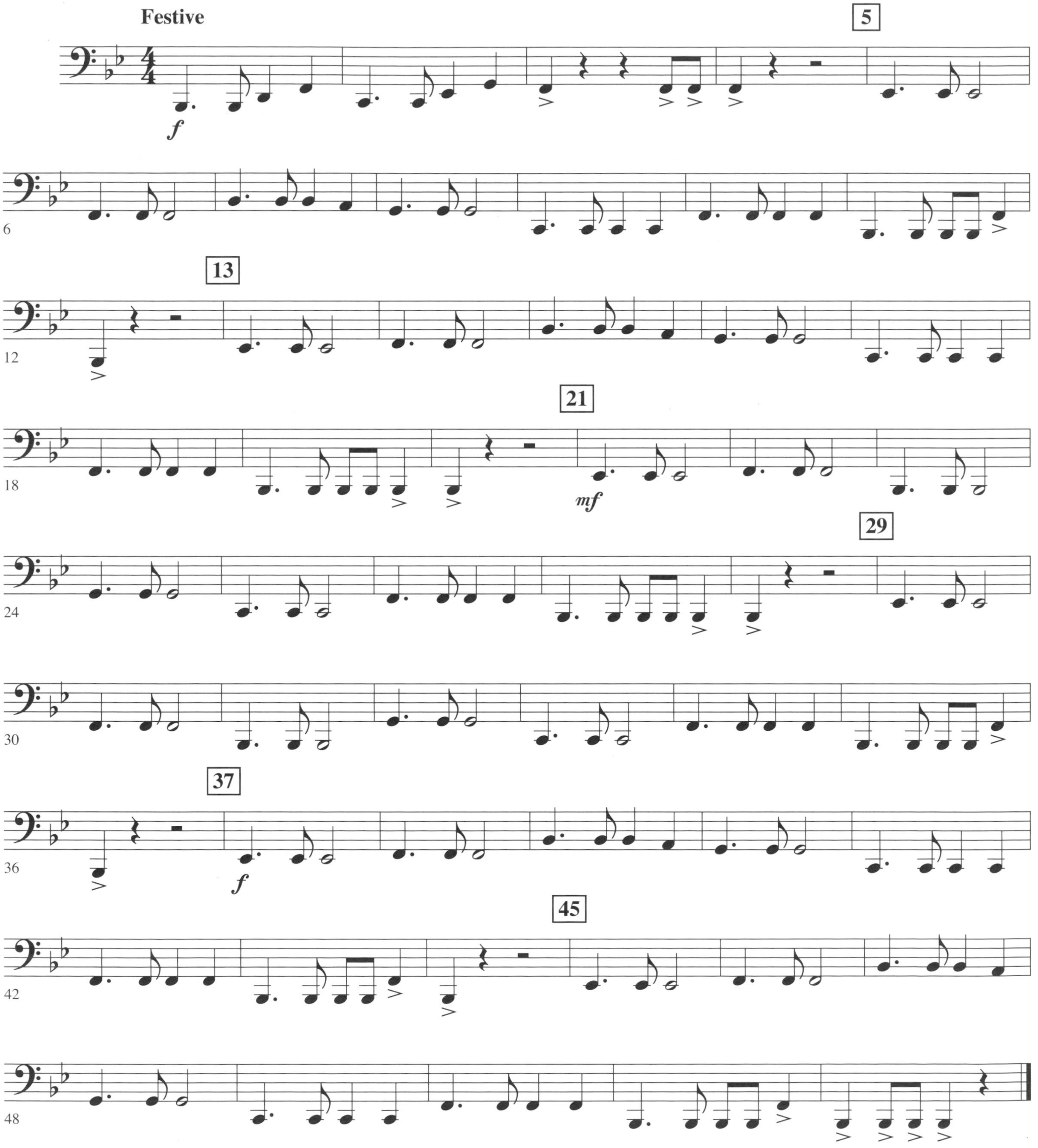

Music and Lyrics by
JOSÉ FELICIANO

Festive

00870018

PARADE OF THE WOODEN SOLDIERS

TUBA
Band Arrangement

English Lyrics by BALLARD MacDONALD
Music by LEON JESSEL
Arranged by PAUL LAVENDER

GOOD KING WENCESLAS

TUBA
Band Arrangement

Words by JOHN M. NEALE
Music from PIAE CANTIONES
Arranged by ROBERT LONGFIELD

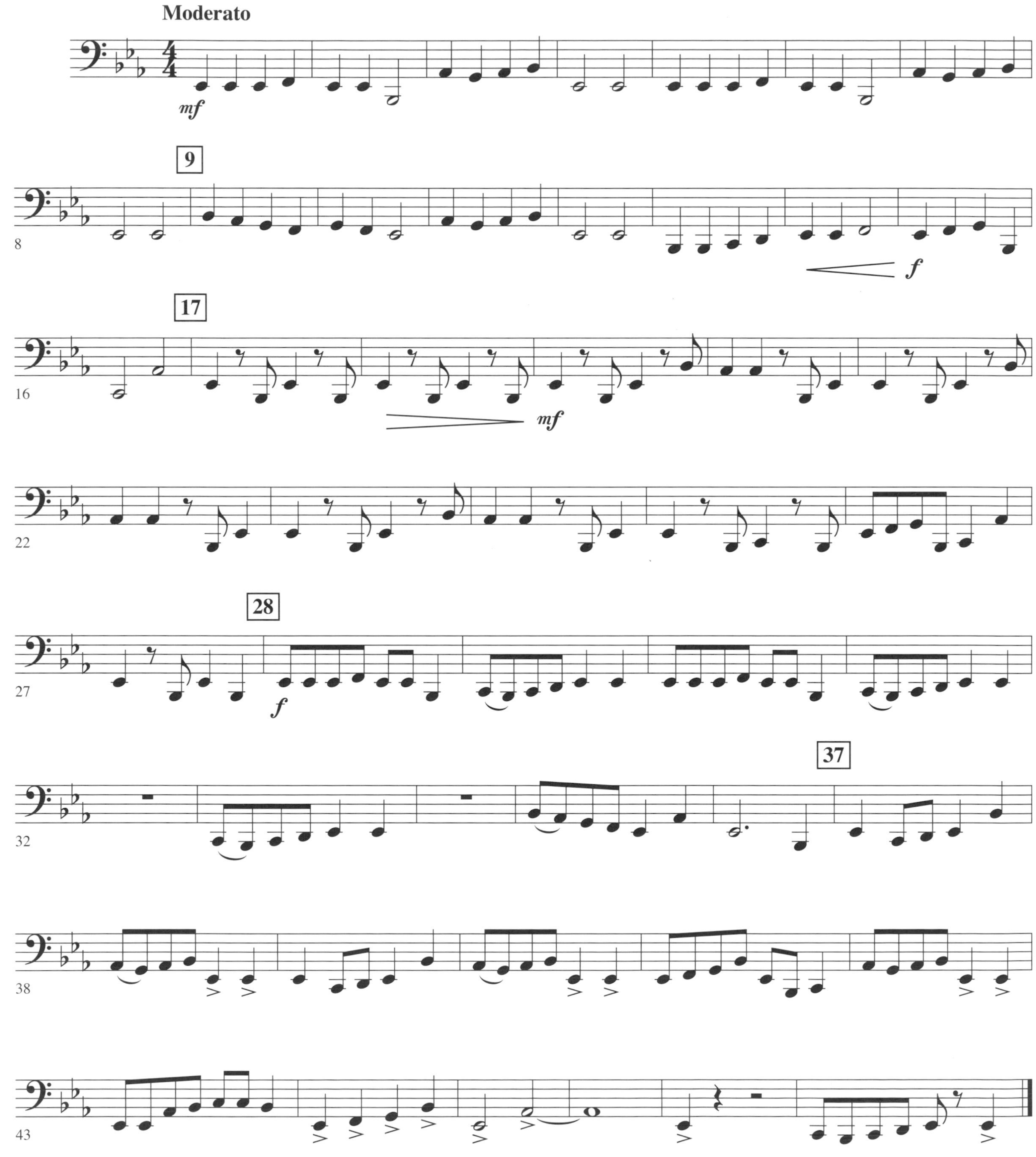

00870018

PAT-A-PAN
(Willie, Take Your Little Drum)

TUBA
Band Arrangement

Words and Music by
BERNARD de la MONNOYE
Arranged by ROBERT LONGFIELD

00870018

SILVER BELLS

TUBA
Band Arrangement

Words and Music by
JAY LIVINGSTON and RAY EVANS
Arranged by PAUL LAVENDER

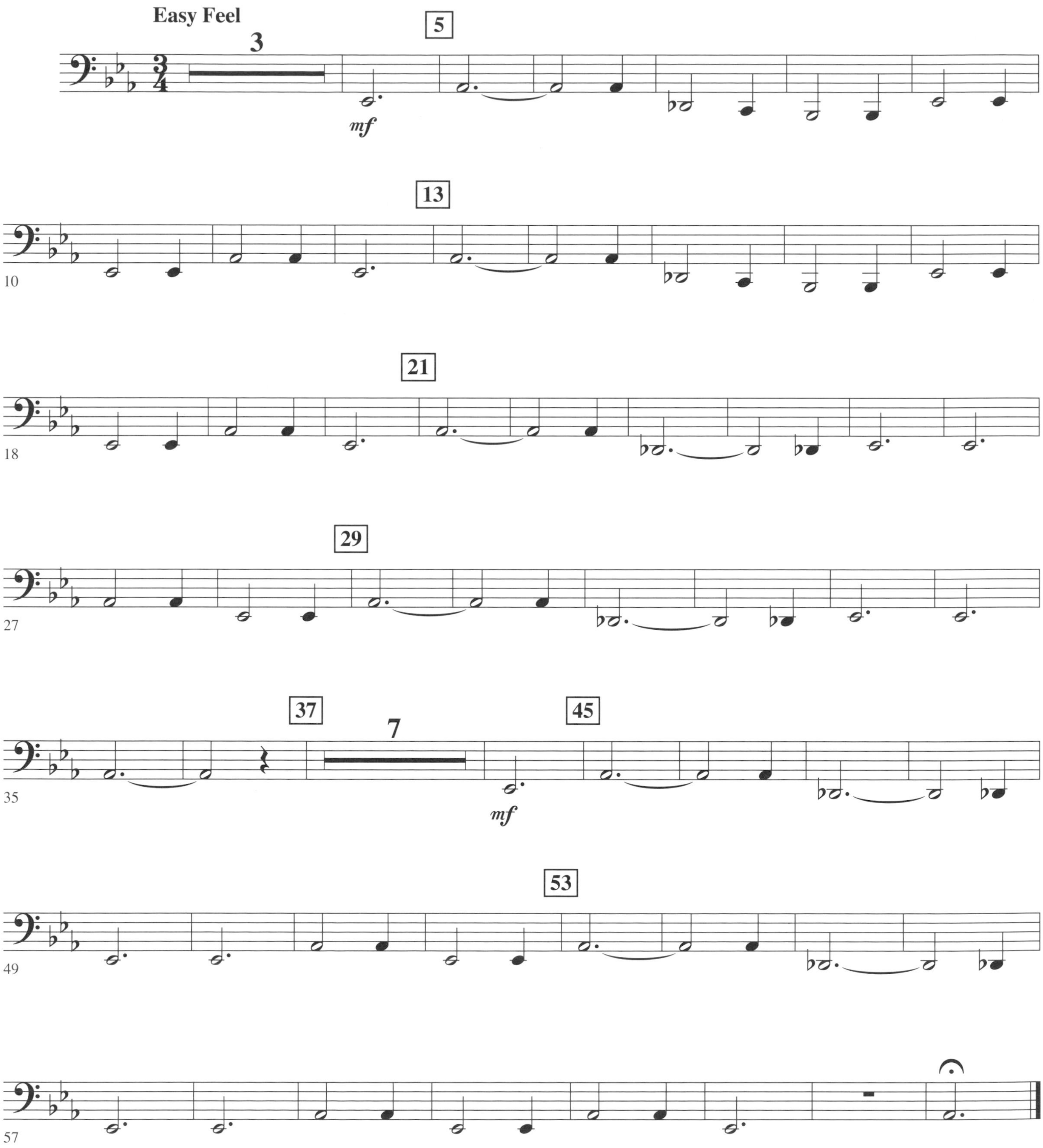

Easy Feel

3 [5]

mf

[13]

10

[21]

18

[29]

27

[37] 7 [45]

35

mf

[53]

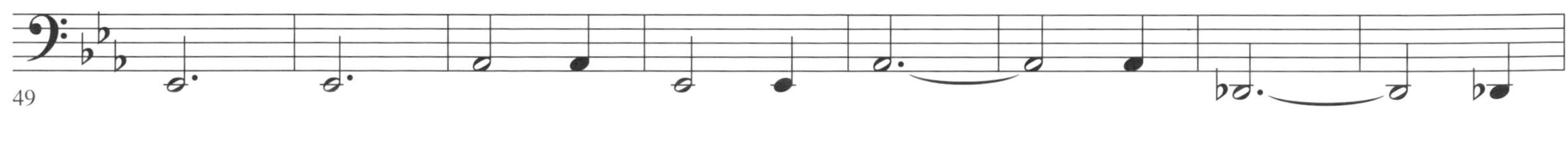

00870018

DO YOU HEAR WHAT I HEAR

TUBA
Band Arrangement

Words and Music by
NOEL REGNEY and GLORIA SHAYNE
Arranged by MICHAEL SWEENEY

From THE SOUND OF MUSIC

MY FAVORITE THINGS

TUBA
Band Arrangement

Lyrics by OSCAR HAMMERSTEIN II
Music by RICHARD RODGERS
Arranged by ROBERT LONGFIELD

00870018

From the Motion Picture Irving Berlin's HOLIDAY INN

WHITE CHRISTMAS

TUBA
Band Arrangement

Words and Music by
IRVING BERLIN
Arranged by JOHNNIE VINSON

CHRISTMAS TIME IS HERE

TUBA
Band Arrangement

Words by LEE MENDELSON
Music by VINCE GUARALDI
Arranged by JOHNNIE VINSON

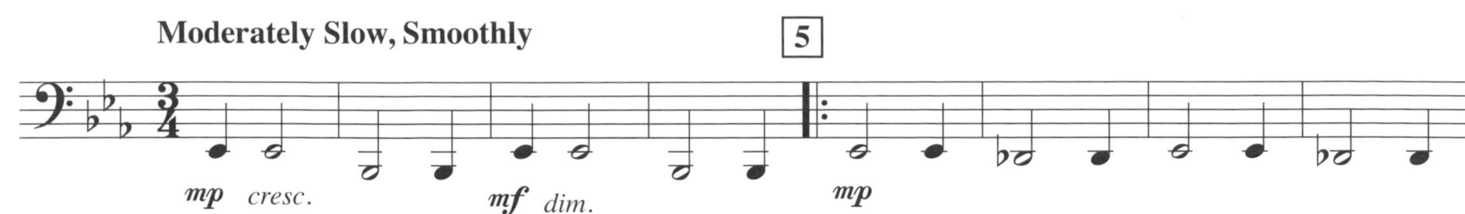

00870018

From Warner Bros. Pictures' THE POLAR EXPRESS

THE POLAR EXPRESS

TUBA
Band Arrangement

Words and Music by
GLEN BALLARD and ALAN SILVESTRI
Arranged by JOHNNIE VINSON